Do You Want a Pet Bearded Dragon?

That's an Odd Pet!

By Louis Mallory

Enslow Publishing

Please visit our website, www.enslow.com. For a free color catalog of all our high-quality books, call toll free 1-800-398-2504 or fax 1-877-980-4454.

Library of Congress Cataloging-in-Publication Data

Names: Mallory, Louis, author.
Title: Do you want a pet bearded dragon? / Louis Mallory.
Description: Buffalo, NY : Enslow Publishing, [2025] | Series: That's an odd pet | Includes bibliographical references and index.
Identifiers: LCCN 2023054157 (print) | LCCN 2023054158 (ebook) | ISBN 9781978540729 (library binding) | ISBN 9781978540712 (paperback) | ISBN 9781978540736 (ebook)
Subjects: LCSH: Bearded dragons (Reptiles) as pets–Juvenile literature.
Classification: LCC SF459.L5 M24 2025 (print) | LCC SF459.L5 (ebook) | DDC 639.3/955–dc23/eng/20231220
LC record available at https://lccn.loc.gov/2023054157
LC ebook record available at https://lccn.loc.gov/2023054158

Published in 2025 by
Enslow Publishing
2544 Clinton Street
Buffalo, NY 14224

Portions of this work were originally authored by Marco Andres and published as *Bearded Dragons*. All new material in this edition is authored by Louis Mallory.

Designer: Claire Zimmermann
Editor: Natalie Humphrey

Photo credits: Cover (photo) Moravian/Shutterstock.com; Series Art (title and heading font, texture) Gleb Guralnyk/Shutterstock.com; Series Art (background retro swirl) ChekmanDaria/Shutterstock.com; Series Art (corner dots) Romanova Ekaterina/Shutterstock.com; Series Art (body text boxes, page number background shape) Angie Makes/Shutterstock.com; Series Art (hand-drawn doodles) yugoro/Shutterstock.com; p. 5 Shinedawn/Shutterstock.com; p. 7 File:Bearded Dragon showing beard.jpg/Wikimedia Commons; p. 9 Ken Griffiths/Shutterstock.com; p. 11 haireena/Shutterstock.com; p. 13 Erin C Matejko/Shutterstock.com; p. 15 smilepoker/Shutterstock.com; p. 17 E. Ast/Shutterstock.com; p. 19 MarekZatko/Shutterstock.com; p. 20 (hand-washing illustration) Noch/Shutterstock.com.

Printed in the United States of America

CPSIA compliance information: Batch #CSENS25. For further information contact Enslow Publishing at 1-800-398-2504.

CONTENTS

Words in the glossary appear in **bold** type the first time they are used in the text.

ODD DRAGONS

A bearded dragon might sound like a strange pet to keep. But these lizards are one of the most popular pet lizards in the United States. Also called beardies, bearded dragons are great pets not only for **experienced** reptile keepers, but for kids too!

JUST THE FACTS!

In the 1960s, Australia made it illegal to **export** wild bearded dragons.

Wild bearded dragons can be found living in Australia. There are around eight different species, or kinds, of bearded dragon. The most common pet beardie is the central bearded dragon.

BEARDIE BODIES

Bearded dragons get their name from the **spikes** on their neck. If a bearded dragon senses danger, it will stand still. Then it will puff out the spiky scales on its throat. This makes the lizard look like it has a big beard!

When a bearded dragon puffs out its throat, its beard may also turn black. This is to make the bearded dragon look more **intimidating** to help it scare away predators.

Male and female bearded dragons can both puff out their throats.

JUST THE FACTS!

Bearded dragons have short legs. However, they can run up to 9 miles (14.5 km) per hour!

COLD-BLOODED

Bearded dragons are reptiles. This means they are cold-blooded. Reptiles use the **temperature** of their surroundings to reach their ideal, or best, body temperature. In the wild, bearded dragons will lay in the sun to keep warm and hide under rocks or dirt to keep cool.

JUST THE FACTS!

Checking on your beardie's color is a good way to make sure your dragon is happy and healthy. If your beardie's skin color changes when the temperature is okay, your beardie may be unhappy or sick!

Bearded dragons also change their skin color depending on the temperature of their surroundings! In the hot desert sun, a bearded dragon's skin turns a lighter color to cool down. When it's cooler outside, the beardie's skin gets darker.

BUYING A BEARDIE

Pet bearded dragons can be purchased at many pet stores. You may also be able to adopt one from a local **animal shelter**. You can also buy a beardie from a private seller. If you do, make sure the business is **reputable** and the seller takes good care of their animals.

JUST THE FACTS!

Some beardie sellers may offer morphs. Morphs are reptiles with colors, shapes, or patterns not usually found in the wild.

No matter where you get your bearded dragon, make sure to ask questions. The more you know about your dragon, the better you'll be able to care for it!

BEARDED DRAGON TANKS

Before you bring your new beardie home, make sure to set up its **tank**. Because bearded dragons are cold-blooded, they need a heat lamp or heating pad to keep warm.

Adult bearded dragons should have a few inches of hard, clay-like sand in the bottom of their tank. Add a piece of wood or rock for your bearded dragon to hide under. Then, add branches to the tank so your dragon can climb and hide.

Two bearded dragons can be kept together if they are of a similar size. It's best to avoid keeping two males or two females together.

JUST THE FACTS!

Bearded dragons can grow up to 24 inches (61 cm) long when they're fully grown. This means adult bearded dragons need big tanks!

DRAGON DIETS

Bearded dragons eat both meat and plants. Crickets are one of their favorite foods. You can buy crickets at the pet store to feed your bearded dragon each day. Younger dragons need to eat more crickets than older ones because they're still growing.

JUST THE FACTS!

If you're not sure what foods to feed your beardie, you can always ask a veterinarian. Veterinarians are animal doctors, and they can help you keep your bearded dragon healthy.

Fruits, vegetables, and bugs should be smaller than the space between your beardie's eyes so your beardie doesn't choke on its food.

Part of your dragon's diet should be fresh fruits and vegetables. Make sure to check which fruits and vegetables are good for your beardie and how often it should get them.

SHEDDING

A few times a year, bearded dragons **shed** their skin. Younger bearded dragons shed their skin more often because they are growing. Shedding beardies might be more **irritable** or tired than usual.

JUST THE FACTS!

Giving your bearded dragon baths can help keep it clean. It can also help a bearded dragon that is already shedding to remove any pieces of skin that may be stuck.

When a bearded dragon is shedding, its eyes might look puffy and its skin color will be dull.

When your bearded dragon is shedding, it's usually best to leave it alone! Make sure your bearded dragon has enough branches and rocks in its tank. Bearded dragons may rub themselves on these to help get the old skin off their bodies.

HOLDING YOUR BEARDIE

Bearded dragons often enjoy being held. To pick up your dragon, carefully slide your hand under its belly. Never hold your pet too tightly or grab it by the legs, tail, or neck. This may scare or hurt your bearded dragon.

Unlike many other small pets, bearded dragons don't need to stay in their tank all the time. Some bearded dragons like to go outside for walks. They may also enjoy car rides.

Some bearded dragons might enjoy playing with toys like balls.

JUST THE FACTS!

Make sure to check on your bearded dragon if you take it out. While most beardies like an adventure outside, some beardies might be **stressed** being outside.

WASH YOUR HANDS!

While your bearded dragon usually won't make you sick, it's important to take care when handling your pet. A bacteria called salmonella can sometimes be found in the waste, or poop, of many lizards. After handling your beardie, make sure to wash your hands.

Bearded dragons can be great pets for people looking for their first lizard. These friendly dragons are easy to handle and care for.

TAKING CARE OF YOUR BEARDIE!

Make sure your bearded dragon's tank is the right size for it. The bigger the beardie, the bigger the tank!

Spot clean your beardie's tank daily and deep clean the tank once a week.

Be gentle when picking up, touching, and handling your beardie.

Bearded dragons would rather live alone.

Bearded dragons can live for at least 10 years with the right care.

Be sure to wash your hands after cleaning, feeding, and handling your pet!

Feed your beardie a diet of fruits, vegetables, and crickets.

JUST THE FACTS!

Handling a bearded dragon once every day for 15 minutes will help it get used to people. As long as your beardie is comfortable, you can hold it longer each time.

GLOSSARY

animal shelter: A place where people take lost animals or animals without an owner.

experienced: Having skills gained by doing something.

export: A good that is sold to another country.

intimidating: Creating a feeling of fear or timidness in a person or animal.

irritable: Easy to anger or annoy.

reputable: Being well thought of, respected, and in good standing.

shed: To get rid of skin, fur, or feathers.

spike: A sharp, pointy thing shaped like a spear or a needle.

stressed: Feeling concerned, worried, or nervous.

tank: A large container, often made of glass, that holds water or other material.

temperature: How hot or cold something is.

FOR MORE INFORMATION

Books

Jaycox, Jaclyn. *Bearded Dragons*. North Mankato, MN: Pebble, 2021.

Szymanski, Jennifer. *Reptiles*. Washington, DC: National Geographic Kids, 2022 .

Websites

Critter Squad: Bearded Dragon Fact Sheet
www.crittersquad.com/fact-sheets/bearded-dragon-fact-sheet/
Learn more facts about bearded dragons.

RSPCA: Caring For Your Bearded Dragon
www.rspca.org.uk/adviceandwelfare/pets/other/beardeddragon
Watch videos and learn more about how to take care of your pet bearded dragon.

Publisher's note to educators and parents: Our editors have carefully reviewed these websites to ensure that they are suitable for students. Many websites change frequently, however, and we cannot guarantee that a site's future contents will continue to meet our high standards of quality and educational value. Be advised that students should be closely supervised whenever they access the internet.

INDEX